Reminiscences of

Captain Robert E. Dornin

U.S. Navy (Retired)

U.S. Naval Institute
Annapolis, Maryland
1987

Preface

Dusty Dornin was one of the real characters of the World War II submarine force. He was a gifted leader--one who made a vivid impression on those with whom he came in contact. Testimony regarding his character and personality are contained in the oral histories of those who had the privilege of serving with him. Dornin also had an impish sense of humor, as the following pages demonstrate. Regrettably, this oral history, which he dictated not long before his death in 1982, is far too brief. He describes only one tour of duty in a career which was distinguished throughout by excellent performance. One wishes that he had covered the entire career through the medium of oral history because the observations in this brief narrative have much to offer the historian.

Paul Stillwell
Director of Oral History
U.S. Naval Institute
August 1987

DECLARATION OF TRUST

The undersigned does hereby appoint and designate as his (her) Trustee herein, the Secretary-Treasurer and Publisher of the United States Naval Institute to perform and discharge the following duties, powers, and privileges in connection with the possession and use of a certain taped interview between the undersigned and the Oral History Department of the United States Naval Institute.

1. Classification of Transcript.

    ( )a. If classified OPEN, the transcript(s) may be read or the recording(s) audited by the qualified personnel upon presentation of proper credentials, as determined by the Secretary-Treasurer of the U.S. Naval Institute.

    ( )b. If classified PERMISSION REQUIRED TO CITE OR QUOTE, the user will be required to obtain permission in writing from the interviewee prior to quoting or citing from either the transcript(s) or the recording(s).

    ( )c. If classified PERMISSION REQUIRED, permission must be obtained in writing from the interviewee before the transcribed interview(s) can be examined or the tape recording(s) audited.

    ( )d. If classified CLOSED, the transcribed interview(s) and the tape recording(s) will be sealed until a time specified by the interviewee. This may be until the death of the interviewee or for any specified number of years.

2. It is expressly understood that in giving this authorization, I am in no way precluded from placing such restrictions as I may desire upon use of the interview at any time during my lifetime, nor does this authorization in any way affect my rights to the copyright of my literary expressions that may be contained in the interview.

Witness my hand and seal this 2 day of June 1972.

I hereby accept and consent to the foregoing Declaration of Trust and the powers therein conferred upon me as Trustee:

Oral History by Captain Robert E. Dornin,
U.S. Navy (Retired)

Place: Captain Dornin's residence in Leucadia, California

Date: 10 May 1982

Subject: Fleet Admiral Ernest J. King

The question has been put to me many times how I was selected to be Admiral King's aide, Admiral King being the head of the largest Navy the world has probably ever seen, one of the sternest, most correct type of admirals.[1]

I have given this much thought and have decided the following. I was a commanding officer of the submarine USS Trigger and had made three very successful war patrols. Prior to that, I had been executive officer of the USS Gudgeon. I made nine war patrols in a row, which is more than par for the course. I was due to be relieved on completing my ninth patrol, which was fairly successful. We had sunk a submarine tender with valuable torpedoes and personnel and the admiral of all the Japanese submarines aboard, plus a destroyer and so forth.

So coming into Pearl, I felt pretty good, and there was everybody down there to welcome me, including Admiral Nimitz.[2] I thought, "What the hell is this?" Well, to

---

[1] Fleet Admiral Ernest J. King, USN, Commander in Chief U.S. Fleet (December 1941 to October 1945) and Chief of Naval Operations (March 1942 to December 1945).
[2] Admiral Chester W. Nimitz, USN, Commander in Chief Pacific Fleet and Commander in Chief Pacific Ocean Areas from December 1941 to November 1945.

make a long story short, Admiral Nimitz invited me up to his house for lunch, which was rather unusual. He proceeded to make me two strong martinis and tell me I had been selected to be Admiral King's aide. Vice Admiral Lockwood was there also.[3] I figured out that they wanted me back there in Washington sitting at the right hand of King, hoping I'd feed the proper information to them about the submarine warfare in the Pacific. So I let them know I wouldn't go. "What? Are you crazy?" one of them asked. So Admiral Nimitz and Admiral Lockwood asked me to go back to the ship, think it over for 24 hours, and then come back and tell them.

I didn't go back to ship; instead, I went to the submarine skippers' lounge in the BOQ and proceeded to have a few beers and give the boys the dope on what had happened.[4] They all said to me, "My God, Dusty, you don't say no to a couple of admirals, much less the Commander in Chief of the Pacific Fleet, Admiral Nimitz. And besides that, we understand that there are 700 women to every able-bodied man back in Washington." I proceeded to give that some thought and decided that maybe the boys had something.

So I accepted the job and then had to wait around for three months before going to Washington. I was not due to relieve until 1 June of 1944. Then I got wondering what in

---

[3] Vice Admiral Charles A. Lockwood, Jr., USN, Commander Submarines Pacific Fleet from February 1943 to December 1945.
[4] BOQ--bachelor officers' quarters

hell Admiral King would want with me. I was only a little over nine years out of the Academy, I was only 31 years old, a lieutenant commander, and had no staff experience. Later on, I found out that Admiral King wanted a bachelor aide around the class of 1935 and one who was a successful submarine skipper. The old man was quite proud of submariners. One time he was the commanding officer of the submarine base in New London. Also, he had five daughters, four of which were married, and the unmarried one, Florie King, was about my age, about 30 years old.

I spent most of the next three months in the San Francisco Bay area, Mill Valley, California, which was my home. I was married there, but I didn't bother to notify anybody in the Navy. So I arrived in Washington and reported on 1 June to relieve Commander Charles Kirkpatrick, a submariner and later the Superintendent of the Naval Academy.[5] When he started briefing me, I said, "Well, the first thing, Kirk, I'd sure like to know where I could live."

He said, "Hell, you can live on the Dauntless, the flagship of the Commander in Chief of the U.S. Fleet." It seemed the old man lived aboard, and there were only four of his personal staff who stood duty on the yacht. He further went on about how much the old man needed some

---

5 Commander Charles C. Kirkpatrick, USN. As a rear admiral, he served as Naval Academy Superintendent from August 1962 to January 1964.

company and also talked about how Admiral King had a daughter who wasn't married and maybe I could see fit to escort her.

I said, "But Kirk, I'm married."

He turned white and he said, "What?"

I said, "I'm married. It's all right with me if my wife can live with us."

And he said, "Oh, shit."

As for the job itself, I personally took care of everything that went in and out of Admiral King's office; all phone calls went through me. Of course, the admiral had a direct line to the President and the Secretary of the Navy.

About three days after I had been there, my buzzer rang, and some fellow told me on the phone, "This is the White House. The President desires the Joint Chiefs of Staff meet General De Gaulle, the head of the provisional French Government, at the Washington airport tomorrow at noon."[6] Admiral King liked a little memo about such matters, so I put one on his desk, and he wrote a little, "Okay." Then I took it back and made the necessary arrangements, ordering the car in front of the Navy Department building, various chiefs of staff and the admiral to be going out to the airport to meet General De Gaulle.

---

[6] General Charles A. De Gaulle, President of the Provisional Government of the French Republic and Commander in Chief French Armies from 1944 to 1946.

About 11:30 the next day, I got kind of itchy and I wondered if he forgot. I was about to go in to remind him when out he came. He was a very tall, handsome, stern man, and he said, "Well, come on. Aren't you coming?" I didn't know that I was to accompany him everywhere he went, but I grabbed my coat and we went down the corridor of the department. Everybody was looking at me as I walked one step to the left of him and one pace behind. We got in the car, and the Marine driver started her up and roared out Constitution Avenue, going about 55. All of a sudden, Admiral King said, "Driver, do you know where you're going?"

The guy said, "No, sir."

With that, Admiral King said, "Turn right here." We almost tipped over on the 14th Street Bridge. The driver now knew we were going to the airport, so he said, "Sirs [he added an 's' to it, by the way], which gate to?"

The old man interrupted and said to me, "I don't know, do you?"

I said, "Yes, sir, hangar six."

With that, he said, "There isn't any hangar six."

I said, "Hell, driver, hangar six." About this time I was hopping goddamn mad, and I remembered that I never wanted the job in the first place.

We drove to hangar six, and I was lucky. I had figured correctly, because one of the dispatchers indicated that any VIPs arriving at the airport under secrecy would go to hangar six. De Gaulle arrived and Admiral King and the Joint Chiefs--General Marshall, General Arnold and Admiral King and Admiral Leahy--were there.[7] Afterward, we got back in the car, which was hot as hell, no air conditioning, and Admiral King didn't say a word.

I went back to the hotel where we were staying temporarily and said to my wife, "Honey, let's go out." I had lasted two more days than I expected to, so I thought we'd go out and have a few drinks. I might add that we had more than a few.

The next morning while I was trying to figure what angles I could pull, my buzzer rang around 9:30 and I said to myself, "Well, here it comes." I went in and stood in front of Admiral King at rigid attention. He peeled off his glasses and looked at me with a little twinkle in his eye. And he said, "Dornin, you and I have to come to an understanding. I didn't want to meet that goddamn Frenchman. I wasn't mad at you yesterday."

With that, I said, "Yes, sir." I understood what he wanted. He didn't want anybody kowtowing to him; you just did your job, and you worked like hell. You could have a lot of fun and feel like you had accomplished something. That's just what happened. It turned out to be a really

---

[7] General George C. Marshall, USA, Army Chief of Staff, 1939-1945; General Henry H. Arnold, USA, Chief of the U.S. Army Air Forces, 1941-1946; Admiral William D. Leahy, USN, chief of staff to the President, 1942-1949.

good relationship. He told me what to do, and to the best of my ability, I did it. But I'd stand up to him if necessary.

Shortly thereafter, Admiral King called me into his office to tell me to arrange for a trip out to Pearl Harbor and then on to Saipan. We had started the invasion of Saipan, and he told me that he wanted to go out there when Saipan was secured by the Marines.[8] On the way back, we would stop by one of our new advance bases. So I made the arrangements. We flew out to Pearl Harbor, picked up Admiral Nimitz, and proceeded toward Saipan. We had word that the Marines had secured the island. The Japs had not surrendered, mind you. But the Marines, always optimistic, said the islands were secured. As we were making our approach to Saipan, we went by the island of Tinian. I saw puffs of smoke, and it looked to me that Japanese artillery was still shelling the island of Saipan, which supposedly had been "secured." We got a percussion shock which shook the hell out of plane, and it scared me. I'll never forget what Admiral King said: "Coming this close, I think, is entirely unnecessary." I could certainly agree.

We landed, and the next day we scheduled a trip to go around the island. You could hear gunfire still going. When the Marines said it was secured, it meant they had it under control and there were supposedly just a few Japanese

---

8 The U.S. invasion of Saipan began on 15 June 1944.

left firing. In the combat zone, high officials normally take off their insignia. But the next day, when King and Nimitz got in the jeep, on their collars were four stars apiece. I got in the back with Admiral Cooke, three stars. The convoy started with three jeeps loaded with Marines, then Admiral King, Admiral Nimitz, and Admiral Turner, the head of the invasion force, and a Marine general followed by the flunkies like myself and Vice Admiral Cooke and so forth.[9]

As we were going up there, we saw that all along the road were dead Japanese soldiers, killed during the banzai attack. The Marines apparently hadn't had time to dispose of the bodies. Then, all of a sudden, gunfire came whisking by us. I knew we were being shot at. The Marines held up their hands to stop the jeeps, then scouted out and flushed out three snipers in a tree in the road just ahead of us. Talk about being scared. I didn't like being shot at. It's all right in a submarine, but not when you're a prime target. I was busy taking off my lieutenant commander insignia, and I said to Vice Admiral Cooke, "Admiral, you'd better do the same. They're going to shoot you first." It was very funny now that I look back on it. We made the tour of the island, and I can tell you one thing. From then on in, King didn't wear his insignia on his collar around Saipan. We were only there about two

---

[9] Vice Admiral Charles M. Cooke, Jr., USN, Admiral King's deputy chief of staff; Vice Admiral Richmond Kelly Turner, USN, Commander Task Force 51.

days, as I recall. Also, when we went back to Pearl Harbor, Nimitz flew in a separate plane.

We left Saipan and proceeded to Majuro. We arrived there, as I recall, early in the morning. A submarine squadron commander was in charge and took Admiral King around for an inspection tour. Vice Admiral Cooke, deputy chief of staff, was a submariner. He said to me, "Hey, Dusty, we don't want to go and see this. We've seen enough submarine bases. See if you can find a bar and open it up and we'll have a brew or two." So that was easy to do, believe me.

We opened the bar, and I'll never forget the bartender, an old chief, who said, "Sir, I've got some 100 proof 40-year-old Old Grand-Dad. How about having that instead of the lousy green beer we got down here?"

We were about finished with our second drink when we happened to glance out the window, and there was Admiral King's barge hightailing it. "Oh, Christ," we thought, because, believe me, when Admiral King arrived in a plane ready to take off, he didn't wait for anybody. By the grace of God, and thanks to the submarine squadron commander, who made an extra fast boat available to us, we caught up to the plane just about the time it was ready to take off. I got in the plane, and just my luck--the only seat left was one alongside Admiral King. So I plumped down, feeling those two 100-proof shots in my belly, and I started yakking and complaining over the fact that it was a hell of a note that of all the present submarine squadron commanders, not one of them had made a war patrol. By this time we had plenty of officers who had made successful war patrols and were senior enough to become Navy captains and squadron commanders. So I proceeded to tell him all this; I was yakking kind of loud, and he told me to shut up. "Oh, brother," I said to myself, "here it comes again." But he added that I should give him a memo on that subject when we got back to Washington. I thought I'd better be quiet.

We got back to Washington, but I didn't put in a memo about this. About three days later, my buzzer rang. When I went into Admiral King's office, he said, "Dornin, where's that memo? I told you to give me one when you returned to Washington about submarine commanders."

I said, "Yes, sir." So I called up Bob Rice, who was in submarine detail at BuPers, and he was just tickled about this.[10] I said Admiral King wanted a list of the squadron commanders that had never made a war patrol. As soon as we got that list, King moved fast. He told me he wanted to see Admiral Jacobs, Chief of the Bureau of Personnel, immediately.[11] When Jacobs arrived, King showed him the list and told him, "I want all these squadron

---

[10] Commander Robert H. Rice, USN; BuPers--Bureau of Naval Personnel
[11] Vice Admiral Randall Jacobs, USN, Chief of the Bureau of Navigation/Naval Personnel from 1941 to 1945.

commanders that haven't made a war patrol relieved, and frankly, I think a lot of them are not too hot." So I did accomplish something for the submarine force.

In the fall of 1944, Army and Navy were number one and number two in the country in football. They both had great teams. Due to the shortage of transportation at that time, Army and Navy were playing each other at either West Point or Annapolis. And whichever one was the visiting team could not have any fans along. By that, I mean the cadets couldn't be down in Annapolis and vice versa. One day Admiral King called me in and said, "Dornin, what do you think about the Army-Navy game? Where could it be played in a large stadium where it involved no transportation? I've got the approval of the President who's all for it to play the game. It's good for the morale of the country to have the number one and two teams in the country play in front of a large audience and have the midshipmen and cadets attend the game."

"I'd go to Baltimore," I told him.

"Baltimore?"

I said, "Hell, yes. The cadets could come down by steamboat and the midshipmen go up from Annapolis by bus."

He said, "That's great." Well, we got the approval of the President. "Now," he said, "notify the Annapolis Superintendent the game is to be played in Baltimore. Start the ball rolling."

I called Admiral Beardall, and he said, "I don't believe it."[12]

"Well," I said, "I have been telling you, Admiral, that Admiral King has the approval of the President that the Army-Navy game be played in Baltimore."

He started hemming and said, "Oh."

I said, "Sir, if you want to call the admiral and question what he asked me to tell you, that's up to you."

"Oh, no," he said, "Oh, no." [They were all scared of Admiral King.] "Okay, thank you so much." Well, this never came out, but that's why the Army-Navy game was played in Baltimore, and I must add that we lost 23 to 7.[13] The bastards knocked out Whitmire on about the second play.[14] He was our great tackle. We lost quite a few other people, and they beat us. That's one of those things.

About the same time, we were having the first landings in the Philippines in Leyte Gulf.[15] I guess things were pretty hot and furious, one thing and another. We were following it, naturally, by dispatches. As we all know, Task Force 38 consisted of all our major carriers, heavy

---

[12] Rear Admiral John R. Beardall, USN, Superintendent of the Naval Academy from January 1942 to August 1945.
[13] The Army-Navy game was played at Baltimore Stadium in 1944. The next year it moved permanently to Philadelphia, where it has been played every year but 1983, when it was played in the Rose Bowl in Pasadena, California.
[14] Midshipman Donald B. Whitmire, USN, an all-American in the class of 1947.
[15] The U.S. invasion of Leyte, led by General Douglas MacArthur, USA, began on 20 October 1944.

cruisers, battleships and so forth and was stationed off San Bernardino Strait to prevent any vast task force of the Japanese from coming down to try to prevent the landings in the Philippines in Leyte Gulf. Well, unfortunately, Halsey's group, Task Force 38, got lured away to the north chasing a very minor Japanese group.[16] With that, the Japanese task group of battleships and cruisers was able to come through San Bernardino Strait and proceed on down to stop the invasion. With Halsey gone, that left our invasion group, the amphibious group, with no air cover, nothing but a few little baby carriers.

Here they were. I happened to have the duty that night on the Dauntless with Admiral King. One thing Admiral King had was an order that he was not to be awakened or disturbed during the night unless the President or Secretary of the Navy wanted to talk to him. Well, about midnight, as I recall, Admiral Dickie Edwards, the number two man in the United States Navy, a four-star admiral, came down and showed me this dispatch and wanted me to show it to Admiral King.[17] And I said, "No, sir, Admiral King does not want to be disturbed."

With that, he looked me in the eye and he said, "Dornin, you're nothing but a damn lieutenant commander. I have four stars. I'm ordering you to show this dispatch to

---

[16] Admiral William F. Halsey, Jr., USN, Commander Third Fleet, June 1944-November 1945.
[17] Admiral Richard S. Edwards, USN, Admiral King's chief of staff.

Admiral King." I had several dispatches coming in, because one of them was from Kinkaid to Halsey, saying that our escort carrier group was being attacked by four battleships and eight cruisers plus others.[18] Kinkaid to Halsey: "Help needed, some heavy ships immediately." And so forth. Finally, Nimitz sent a message to Halsey: "Where, repeat, where is Task Force 38? The world wonders."[19] So I went in and switched on the light. Admiral King opened up one eye like an eagle's eye, and I handed him these few dispatches. He looked at them and then said, "Just what in hell do you want me to do about it, Dornin, at midnight? What do you think I've got Nimitz out there for? Now get out!"

With that, I turned around and said, "Yes, sir." I knew that this short outburst was not directed at me. Well, I left the cabin, and by the time I got to the cabin door, Admiral Edwards apparently had run off the ship, because I couldn't see him anywhere.

Nothing happened for about two days, fortunately. The Japanese for some unknown reason left the area and the invasion was successful. But about two or three days later, when Task Force 38 had come back to anchor and replenish and so forth, my buzzer rang. I went in to see

---

18 Vice Admiral Thomas C. Kinkaid, USN, Commander Allied Naval Forces Southwest Pacific and Commander U.S. Seventh Fleet from October 1943 to November 1945.
19 For background on this 25 October 1944 message, see Nimitz by E.B. Potter (Annapolis, Maryland: Naval Institute Press, 1976.)

Admiral King, and he said, "I want to see Admiral Halsey immediately."

"Yes, sir."

With that, I called Vice Admiral Jacobs and told him Admiral King wanted to see Admiral Halsey immediately. He said, "Well, he's out in Ulithi Atoll."

I said, "Sir, I'm only carrying out Admiral King's order."

Admiral Jacobs knew Admiral King well, so he said, "Okay, Dornin."

In a short time, believe me, a very short time, Admiral Halsey showed up and came into the office. I knew him from way back. I was an ex-football player. Halsey was quite a football player himself.

He said, "How are you, Dusty?"

I said, "Just a minute, sir, I'll tell Admiral King you're here." So I went and told Admiral King.

Admiral King said, "Show him in." I had hardly gotten out of the door, but I'm telling you, you talk about reprimands, bawling outs--when you hear a fleet admiral rip up and down on another four-star admiral, boy, it was insulting, not foul, but the devil's language. I never heard anything in the world like it. I couldn't help but hear it. As a matter of fact, I think everybody on the second deck of the Navy Department heard him. Well, anyway, it was something. King was very fond of Halsey, but he wanted perfection and frankly, Halsey made a hell of a blunder, and it could have been very costly.

I could go on for some time, since I attended with Admiral King many conferences in the Pacific and such other international conferences at Malta, Yalta, Quebec. I think I'd like to wind this up by telling a little about Potsdam.[20] That was held, of course, in Berlin right after the Germans capitulated.

At that time, Truman had taken over the Presidency, and Churchill at the commencement of the exercise was still Prime Minister.[21] Well, there were a lot of big things. The Russians had agreed to come in the war against Japan three months after the Germans had surrendered unconditionally. So here we were, and we were reading the Japanese dispatches right and left; we were breaking their codes. We knew that they had made overtures through the Swiss Embassy to the Russians--after all, the Russians and the Japanese were still at peace--to intercede on the Japanese behalf for a surrender. Not an unconditional one but a surrender because the Third Fleet and the Fifth Fleet were cruising up and down their coast in bombing aircraft raids indiscriminately. The B-29s with their fire bombs from Saipan had practically burned out Tokyo and the

---

[20] American, British, and Soviet leaders met in Potsdam (now part of East Germany) over 17 July-2 August 1945 to discuss the preliminary details of the administration of Germany.
[21] Sir Winston Churchill, Prime Minister from May 1940 to July 1945.

submarines had strangled their only pipeline for oil or any needed imports. So there they were--they were starving to death and there was nothing left. It had been decided to invade Kyushu on 1 November. Now mind you, this is way back in July. So at this time, the conference came to a halt because Churchill was defeated and was relieved by Attlee, which caused delay.[22] We sat around and didn't do anything for about three days until the new Prime Minister came.

At that time, they had also, of course, dropped the first nuclear test bombs which had been successful, a couple of bombs were en route to Saipan to drop on Japan if necessary. Well, it just didn't seem right whether we should or not, because here we had the Japs on the ropes and everything was starting to go the other direction. Very few American lives would be lost, because there was no more fighting to be done--that is, land fighting. They decided to just starve them to death so they would ask for unconditional surrender. Well, I do know how Admiral King felt. We had them on their knees and why not wait for three or four months and then if they didn't, drop the bomb. I mean, why do it now? After all, we really weren't dropping them on major military targets. I know he was against dropping it, but meanwhile the Russians, knowing full well (the darn catch was that they knew) that once we

---

[22] Earl Clement R. Attlee, Prime Minister from 1945 until 1951, when Churchill was again put into office.

did, hell, Japan would surrender unconditionally to us and then Japan would only deal with us.

So lo and behold, as I recall, one or two days right before we dropped the atomic bomb, the Russians invaded Japan. Of course, we all know the results. Japan immediately capitulated, surrendered unconditionally. The Russians meanwhile had gobbled up a lot of territory and were able to sit in and play a part in the surrender of Japan and more or less get a hell of a lot they didn't deserve. My point is Admiral King felt we could lick them alone; why give them a chance and why drop the bomb at all at that time? I don't know. I do know that he was overruled. I don't know at what level. General Marshall and he saw eye to eye.[23] I know Admiral Leahy did, too.[24] I don't know about General Arnold, whose plane carried the bomb.[25] But whenever you didn't have a unanimous decision on the Joint Chiefs of Staff, you went to the President. Now, who makes the decision? I do know. Admiral King said, "I don't think we should do it at this time. It is not necessary." So I wonder. And who will ever know? That's Monday morning quarterbacking. Who will ever regret dropping that bomb after all? I don't think the Orientals, the Asians, you name it, will ever forgive us. It's just

---

[23] General of the Army George C. Marshall, USA, U.S. Army Chief of Staff from 1939-1945.
[24] Fleet Admiral William D. Leahy, USN, Chairman of the Joint Chiefs of Staff.
[25] General of the Army Henry H. Arnold, USA, Commander of U.S. Air Forces.

one of those things. We were the first and only people to drop the bomb. Who knows? Maybe someday we will regret it. Again, that's the second Monday morning quarterback.

Right after the war, Admiral King was relieved in December by Admiral Nimitz, and I became Admiral Nimitz's aide for about three or four months. Both great mean, but King taught me so much--to be able to delegate authority. Once you delegate it, trust the people, be firm, and demand the best of everybody. I'll never forget him telling me, "I always try to get somebody that can do a better job in that particular position than I could do it. And then, by God, let him do it and don't, for goodness sakes, don't keep bitching on what he does; thank him."

Index

to

Reminiscences of

Captain Robert E. Dornin

U.S. Navy (Retired)

Air Forces, U.S. Army
   Allied B-29 raids on Tokyo from Saipan in 1945 were highly effective, page 16

Army-Navy Football Game
   Dornin engineered move of 1944 game to Baltimore, pages 11-12; Army win in 1944, page 12

Atomic Bomb
   Many top U.S. military leaders were opposed to bombing Japan in July 1945, feeling that country could be defeated with conventional warfare, pages 17-18

Attlee, Earl Clement R.
   Election as Prime Minister in mid-1945 delays Potsdam Conference, page 17

B-29 Bombers
   Allied B-29 raids on Tokyo from Saipan in 1945 were highly effective, page 16

Baltimore, Maryland
   Dornin engineered move of 1944 Army-Navy football game to Baltimore, pages 11-12; Army win in 1944, page 12

Beardall, Rear Admiral John R., USN (USNA, 1908)
   Naval Academy Superintendent balked when told that 1944 Army-Navy game would be played in Baltimore, page 12

Churchill, Sir Winston
   Defeat in Prime Minister re-election bid in mid-1945 delayed Potsdam Conference, page 7

Codebreaking
   Through U.S. codebreaking success with Japanese message traffic by 1945, Allies were aware of overtures made to Russians for surrender, page 16

Cooke, Vice Admiral Charles M., Jr., USN (USNA, 1910)
   Chief of Naval Operations Deputy Chief of Staff removed collar insignia during mid-1944 Saipan trip, page 8; while drinking with Dornin on Majuro in mid-1944, almost missed Chief of Naval Operations's plane, page 9

Dauntless, USS (PG-61)
   Admiral King expected his new "bachelor" aide, Dornin, to live on board, pages 3-4; Dornin, on duty in Dauntless, ordered to wake his boss with news about Leyte Gulf action in late 1944, pages 13-14

De Gaulle, General Charles A.
   Visit to Washington in 1944 to meet with the Joint Chiefs caused problems for Dornin when Admiral King dragged his feet, pages 4-6

Dornin, Captain Robert E., USN (USNA, 1935)
  Successes as executive officer of Gudgeon (SS-211) and commanding officer of Trigger (SS-237) led to selection as Admiral King's aide in 1944, page 1; marriage in spring 1944 foiled Admiral King's preference of a bachelor aide, pages 3-4; family, pages 3-4, 6; duties as aide to Chief of Naval Operations King, pages 4-16, 19; relationship with Admiral King, pages 6-7, 19

Edwards, Admiral Richard S., USN (USNA, 1907)
  As Chief of Naval Operations King's chief of staff in late 1944, demanded that aide Dornin wake his boss with Leyte Gulf news despite King's strict instructions not to be disturbed, pages 13-14

Halsey, Admiral William F., Jr., USN (USNA, 1904)
  Decision to move Task Force 38 from San Bernardino Strait before late 1944 Leyte Gulf invasion angered Chief of Naval Operations King, pages 12-16

Insignia
  Admiral King and other officers removed collar insignia as safety precaution at Saipan in mid-1944, page 8

Jacobs, Vice Admiral Randall, USN (USNA, 1907)
  Chief of the Bureau of Naval Personnel ordered in 1944 to replace submarine squadron commanders who had not made a war patrol, pages 10-11; told by Chief of Naval Operations King to fetch Third Fleet Commander Halsey after muddled Leyte Gulf action in late 1944, page 15

Japan
  Success at Leyte Gulf in late 1944 brought Chief of Naval Operations King's wrath in Third Fleet Commander Halsey, pages 12-16; attempted to arrange surrender through Soviet Union in 1945, page 16; B-29 raids on Tokyo from Saipan in 1945, page 16; discussion of decision to drop atomic and nuclear bombs, pages 17-18

Joint Chiefs of Staff (JCS)
  JCS split on decision to drop atomic bomb on Japan in July 1945, page 18

King, Fleet Admiral Ernest J., USN (USNA, 1901)
  Dornin's thoughts on his selection as Admiral King's aide in 1944, pages 1, 3; wanted bachelor aide, pages 3-4; attitude towards General De Gaulle, pages 4-6; trip to Saipan in mid-1944, pages 7-9; removed collar insignia for safety from snipers at Saipan, page 8; toured submarine base at Majuro in mid-1944, page 9; aide Dornin's slightly inebriated complaint to King about unseasoned submarine squadron commanders eventually resulted in changes, pages 10-11; changes site of 1944 Army-Navy game to Baltimore, pages 11-12; viewed by other

officers, page 12; reaction to disappointing action in Leyte Gulf in late 1944, pages 12-16; against dropping atomic bomb on Japan, pages 17-18; philosophy on delegating authority, page 19

Kinkaid, Vice Admiral Thomas C., USN (USNA, 1908)
Aide Dornin woke Chief of Naval Operations King in late 1944 with messages from Commander Seventh Fleet Kinkaid to Commander Third Fleet Halsey concerning Leyte Gulf action, page 14

Kirkpatrick, Commander Charles C., USN (USNA, 1931)
Dornin's predecessor as aide to Chief of Naval Operations King flustered in the spring of 1944 when he found out Dornin had recently been married, pages 3-4

Kyushu
At Potsdam Conference in mid-1945, decision was made to invade Kyushu on 1 November, page 17

Leahy, Fleet Admiral William D., USN (USNA, 1897)
As Chairman of the Joint Chiefs of Staff in July 1945, in agreement with Chief of Naval Operations King that the war with Japan could be ended with conventional means, page 18

Leyte Gulf, Battle of
Chief of Naval Operations King's reaction to news of Admiral William Halsey's actions in late 1944, pages 12-16

Majuro
While Chief of Naval Operations King toured submarine base here, Vice Admiral Cooke and Dornin went drinking and almost missed plane home, page 9

Marine Corps, U.S.
Saipan, supposedly secured by the Marines, still presented dangers to high-ranking visitors in mid-1944, pages 7-8

Marshall, General George C., USA
Army Chief of Staff in agreement with Chief of Naval Operations King against dropping atomic bomb, page 18

Military Academy, U.S.
Army-Navy football game moved to Baltimore in 1944 to permit attendance by cadets, pages 11-12

Naval Academy, U.S.
Army-Navy football game moved to Baltimore in 1944 to permit attendance by cadets, pages 11-12

Nimitz, Admiral Chester W., USN (USNA, 1905)
Greeted Dornin upon return to Pearl Harbor after war patrol and told him over lunch that his next billet would be as aide to Admiral King, pages 1-2; trip to Saipan with Admiral King in mid-1944, pages 7-9; Chief of Naval Operations King's faith in

Commander in Chief U.S. Pacific Fleet Nimitz was demonstrated during late 1944 Leyte Gulf action, page 14; Dornin served briefly as Nimitz's aide when he became Chief of Naval Operations in December 1945, page 19

Nuclear Weapons
   Nuclear bombs sent to Saipan in mid-1945 for potential use on Japan, page 17

Pearl Harbor
   Admiral King and Dornin flew to Pearl Harbor on way to Saipan in mid-1944, page 7

Potsdam Conference (17 July-2 August 1945)
   Decision made to invade Kyushu on 1 November, page 17; conference delayed when churchill defeated and replaced by Attlee, page 17

Rice, Commander Robert H., USN (USNA, 1927)
   Submarine detailer in 1944 thrilled by action taken by Admiral King that required squadron commanders to have combat experience, page 10

Saipan
   Admiral King, Admiral Nimitz, and Dornin made precarious trip to this island after the Marines had supposedly secured it in mid-1944, pages 7-9; in 1945, Allied B-29 raids on Tokyo from Saipan were very effective, page 16; nuclear bombs sent to Saipan in summer of 1945 for use on Japan, page 17

Soviet Union
   Through codebreaking efforts, U.S. aware that Japan had approached Soviets about a surrender by mid-1945, page 16; underhanded in invading Japan right before U.S. planned to drop atomic bomb in July 1945, pages 17-18

Squadron Command - Submarine
   Dornin's inebriated complaint in mid-1944 to Chief of Naval Operations King about squadron commanders who were in charge without ever having been on a war patrol eventually got results, pages 10-11

Task Force 38
   Admiral Halsey's decision to divert this unit to north of Leyte Gulf in late 1944 had unfortunate results, pages 12-16

Tinian
   As Admirals King and Nimitz and Dornin approached Saipan by air in mid-1944, they saw signs of the Japanese shelling the island from Tinian, page 7

www.ingramcontent.com/pod-product-compliance
Lightning Source LLC
Chambersburg PA
CBHW081521220426
43209CB00102B/1375